A STEP-BY-STEP BOOK ABOUT
SNAKES

ROBERT ANDERSON

Photography:
Robert Anderson, Robert W. Applegate, Dr. Guido Dingerkus, F. J. Dodd, John Dommers, Dr. Marcos Freiberg, Jeff Gee, Richard L. Holland, Burkhard Kahl, Alex Kerstitch, James K. Langhammer, Ken Lucas, Steinhart Aquarium, Gerhard Marcuse, Dr. Sherman A. Minton, Louis Porras, P. J. Stafford, W. Tomey, A. van den Nieuwenhuizen.
Humorous illustrations by Andrew Prendimano.

© **1987 by T.F.H. Publications, Inc.**

Distributed in the UNITED STATES by T.F.H. Publications, Inc., 211 West Sylvania Avenue, Neptune City, NJ 07753; in CANADA to the Pet Trade by H & L Pet Supplies Inc., 27 Kingston Crescent, Kitchener, Ontario N2B 2T6; Rolf C. Hagen Ltd., 3225 Sartelon Street, Montreal 382 Quebec; in CANADA to the Book Trade by Macmillan of Canada (A Division of Canada Publishing Corporation), 164 Commander Boulevard, Agincourt, Ontario M1S 3C7; in ENGLAND by T.F.H. Publications Limited, 4 Kier Park, Ascot, Berkshire SL5 7DS; in AUSTRALIA AND THE SOUTH PACIFIC by T.F.H. (Australia) Pty. Ltd., Box 149, Brookvale 2100 N.S.W., Australia; in NEW ZEALAND by Ross Haines & Son, Ltd., 18 Monmouth Street, Grey Lynn, Auckland 2, New Zealand; in SINGAPORE AND MALAYSIA by MPH Distributors (S) Pte., Ltd., 601 Sims Drive, #03/07/21, Singapore 1438; in the PHILIPPINES by Bio-Research, 5 Lippay Street, San Lorenzo Village, Makati Rizal; in SOUTH AFRICA by Multipet Pty. Ltd., 30 Turners Avenue, Durban 4001. Published by T.F.H. Publications, Inc. Manufactured in the United States of America by T.F.H. Publications, Inc.

Contents

FACTS ABOUT SNAKES

Snakes are limbless reptiles, and most have long, slender, almost cylindrical bodies. They have fused transparent eyelids and ears that are without drums or external cavities. They have a retractile forked tongue. Their dorsal surface and sides are covered with many rows of overlapping scales, and the ventral or belly surface is covered by a single row of broad scales called belly scales, ventral plates, or scutes.

Little is known about the origin of snakes. Fossils of the oldest known snake date from Lower Cretaceous times, about 125 million years ago.

Like all reptiles, snakes are cold-blooded creatures. The term cold-blooded simply means that the snake's blood is usually not much higher in temperature than the surrounding air. This explains why they are generally more active on warm, sunny days and sluggish during cold weather. The snakes that live in northern regions have to go underground and hibernate during the winter months. When a snake hibernates and the body temperature is lowered, all of the body processes are slowed down, including the heartbeat. Hibernation is a sort of suspended animation.

At first thought, one is likely to feel a little sorry for the snake that is without arms or legs—it appears to be under a most discouraging handicap in the eternal struggle for survival. In reality, however, the snake needs no sympathy, for it is found to have a highly complex structure in compensation that makes it the most successful of all the reptiles.

Snakes have adapted themselves to a variety of conditions. Some species can climb trees and are able to move about with great speed through the interlocking branches. Others make their homes in or near salt, brackish, or fresh bodies of water and can dive and swim with such expertness that they are able to catch a swimming fish. Some snakes are able to burrow underground and lead a more or less subterranean existence, much like the earthworms. The sea snakes

FACING PAGE: The most colorful snakes are not always the best pets. Beginners should stay away from expensive imports like this young green tree python, *Chondropython viridis*.

have even gone so far as to develop flattened, rudder-like tails. Some species spend their entire life at sea, while others come ashore only for the purpose of laying their eggs. The great majority of snakes, however, live on the ground, but all of them are able to swim, many can climb, and quite a few can burrow to some extent.

There are more than 2,000 distinct species of snakes living today. They are well distributed throughout the world and range vertically from below sea level to at least 14,000 feet (4300 meters) above sea level. However, some islands are without native snakes, among them the Azores, Ireland, New Zealand, and the Hawaiian Islands. Their range in North America extends northward to the 60th parallel.

Snakes vary in size and general appearance as much as any other group of animals. The giant semiaquatic anaconda of South America measures as much as three feet (one meter) in circumference and is known as the largest snake of the New World. The reticulated python of Asia has been recorded up to 32 feet (9.8 meters) in length and is probably the longest snake in the world. The diminutive worm snake is the smallest snake found in eastern North America. The eastern species measures 7½ to 11 inches (19 to 28 cm). This small snake is often described as a serpentine imitation of the common earthworm.

Typhlops braminus is an Old World blind worm snake whose small size allows it to become widely introduced in the roots of plants. Females of this species can apparently produce young without mating. Snakes that are always burrowing make poor pets.

Even smaller is the worm-like Texas blind snake, which reaches a maximum of 27 cm, less than 11 inches. Some of the tree and vine snakes are tremendously elongated, slender, almost string-like serpents. Many of the poisonous vipers are short and stout.

Some common snakes exhibit bright scarlet and yellow bands. Many tropical species display beautiful patterns of rich colors, while others are modestly colored in somber grays and blacks.

Although snakes may be characterized as animals with a head and long body, there are actually four parts to their entire struc-

Snakes banded in bright colors should never be handled by a beginner because too many are venomous. This is an Arizona coral snake, *Micruroides euryxanthus.*

ture: a head, neck, trunk, and tail. In the majority of forms the underside is flattened, but in some, especially the burrowing snakes, the body is quite cylindrical.

As mentioned earlier, a snake's skin is covered with scales and plates. The scales may be smooth or they may be keeled, that is, provided with a ridge down the middle. The water snakes and rattlesnakes are typical examples of those with keeled scales. The kingsnakes and the racers are good examples of smooth-scaled species. The scales are neither wet nor slimy.

All snakes shed their outer layer of skin during the warm

A snake's colors are at their best after it has shed. This boa constrictor shows a great deal of iridescence in its color pattern.

months (throughout the year in the extreme southern states), and these discarded paper-thin skins are often found among rock piles and low brush. For a few days before this event the snake becomes listless, its overall color becomes dull, and a bluish white film appears over the eyes. The snake begins the process of shedding by rubbing its chin against a rough rock or sharp branch until the outer skin or epidermis splits and loosens about the head, after which the reptile literally crawls out of it, turning it inside out as it does so. The shed skin is a perfect replica of the snake, the most minute detail of all the scales being accurately retained. The new skin that is formed under the old one is rich in color. Even the eyes shed their outer covering and emerge clear and bright.

When we observe a snake crawling on the ground we find that it does so with effortless ease and satisfactory progress. Snakes have several methods of locomotion. The ventral scales, plates, or scutes of a snake overlap one another, with the free edges directed toward the tail. Since each is overlapped by the one in front of it, they all slip easily over any irregularities of the ground. Many of the thick-

bodied snakes, such as the pythons and vipers, crawl in a perfectly straight line by pressing the scutes in certain parts of their body against the ground and then moving the body forward by muscular action. This form of locomotion is termed rectilinear movement. Slender snakes, such as the rat snakes and racers, are not capable of rectilinear movement. These snakes progress by a sinuous movement where each curve of their body is pressed against surface irregularities. This form of locomotion is termed serpentine motion. Thick-bodied snakes when in a hurry are capable of serpentine motion. Most snakes find it almost impossible to progress when placed on a smooth surface such as glass that offers them no anchor for their scutes. However, some desert snakes are capable of a side-winding motion that enables them to glide on the smooth surface of glass as well as loose sand.

Despite the fact that snakes are without eardrums and external ear cavities, they make up for this deficiency by being remarkably sensitive to odors and certain vibrations. The forked tongue that is incessantly flicked in and out of the mouth is an organ to aid the snake's ability to smell. The delicate tips of the tongue are lightly touched to objects in the snake's path or waved in the air. They carry back minute particles to where they are lodged into two small cavities in the roof of the mouth. These cavities contain delicate sense organs that are collectively termed Jacobson's organ.

All snakes are carnivorous, and in a wild state most prefer living prey. Some water snakes, however, will feed on dead fish, frogs, and crayfish. Captive snakes will often take dead mice, fish, and even strips of raw meat. The snake's jaws are usually long and well supplied

Like many other animals whose ancestors were burrowers, snakes have lost the external ear. A snake detects vibrations through the ground, however, and is not really deaf.

with sharp teeth that point back in the direction of the throat. There are no molars for grinding, and therefore all prey must be swallowed whole. Except for the species where some of the teeth are modified for injecting venom, the only function of the snake's teeth is to seize and hold the reptile's prey while it is being swallowed. To overcome struggling prey, snakes have developed several methods of behavior. The constrictors wrap a coil or two about their prey and squeeze it until suffocated, at which time the snake will swallow it, usually head first. Other snakes simply press the prey against the ground with a

This slender African boomslang, *Dispholidus typus,* is able to swallow a lizard that is much wider than the snake's diameter.

loop of their body and hold it there while swallowing it. Most poisonous species strike their prey and inject a dose of venom or grab and chew for several minutes. Swallowing is then delayed until the victim is unconscious or dead. Some venomous snakes are also constrictors (the Indian cobra is a good example), but even these depend mostly upon their venom to subdue their prey. Most prey is usually swallowed head first to avoid the resistance of scales, feathers, and limbs.

The jaws of a snake are different from those of all other living vertebrates. The snake's jaws do not form rigid units but are separated at the extreme front by an elastic ligament so that the snake has four separate and more or less independently movable jaws. In grasping prey for the process of swallowing, the snake secures a firm grip on the animal's nose. One side of the lower jaw is then pushed forward while the other side of the lower jaw remains fixed; the elastic ligament makes this possible. After the recurved teeth on the forward side of the jaw have been imbedded in the head of the prey, the other side of the lower jaw slides up even with the forward side. At this time

the upper jaws creep forward, one at a time. The entire operation continues, first the two lower jaw sides and then the two upper jaw sides, time and time again until the prey is completely engulfed, at which time the throat muscles contract to complete the swallowing process.

Many snakes reproduce by laying eggs and are said to be oviparous. Other snakes produce living young and are termed ovoviviparous. Some of these snakes merely retain the eggs in their body until they hatch. Snake eggs are generally elongate, white or grayish white in color, and covered with a tough leather-like shell. The egg of a snake becomes larger and darker in color as the baby snake develops. Snakes usually deposit their eggs under rotting logs, in decaying vegetation, or in some other moderately moist location. The young snake is provided with a sharp growth on its nose called an egg tooth, with which it ruptures the shell when ready to emerge. This egg tooth is then lost. In the great majority of species the mother takes no interest in the eggs after they are laid, but goes her own way leaving the eggs and young strictly on their own. Hatchlings as well as the young of ovoviviparous snakes are all independent from the start. The poisonous species are born fully equipped with fangs and a supply of venom and are capable of administering a dangerous bite. The constricting snakes are able to overpower prey within the compass of their size, and other species are all well prepared to take to the business of living entirely on their own resources

This European water snake, *Natrix natrix*, lays eggs, while its close relatives in North America, *Nerodia* species, give live birth.

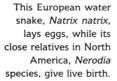

SNAKES AS PETS

It is hard to say exactly which snake makes the best pet. However, there are a couple of outstanding points to keep in mind: gentleness and ease of feeding.

Some snakes that may be considered as being good pets by some experienced fanciers may be unsuitable for the average beginner because of difficulties in feeding and untamable behavior. If you keep a snake that continues to bite when you want to handle it or clean its cage, it is equally as discouraging as keeping one that refuses to eat.

Probably the most gentle and best feeding snakes are those that feed on earthworms. Earthworms are available throughout the spring and summer months, and they can be cultivated with very little care during the cold fall and winter months. The red manure worms are toxic and should never be fed to your snakes. Nightcrawlers of various sizes are excellent and should be the only kind of earthworms used to feed your snakes. Worms may be made available by watering your lawn after dark. The worms will come to the surface of the ground and can be hunted with the aid of a flashlight.

My choice for the beginner is a half-grown garter snake because it is a very common snake, easy to find, easy to catch, tames quickly, is a hardy feeder, and acclimates itself quickly to temperature and humidity changes. Garter snakes can often be found under all kinds of debris during the hot days of summer and under debris covered by the first snow during the mid-fall season. Garter snakes emit a strong-smelling musk when first captured but will not continue to do so after they have been handled for a while. Another advantage of the garter snake is that it will breed in captivity and the young will feed on small nightcrawlers. A garter snake will also feed off small frogs.

Fish-eating snakes (water snakes) are usually easy to keep because most are excellent feeders and fish of one kind or another is available all year around. The objection to beginners keeping these snakes, however, is that most species are ill-tempered and capable of

FACING PAGE: Corn snakes, *Elaphe guttata*, and common kingsnakes, *Lampropeltis getulus*, are among the best pet snakes for beginners. They are available in many color forms. This is a corn snake.

delivering a very severe, painful, skin-lacerating bite. All bites should be treated immediately with a good antiseptic. It is recommended that the handler use a good pair of soft canvas or leather work gloves.

Water snakes can gradually be trained to take dead fish or strips of fish. When being fed to your snake, the fish should be held with plastic or wooden photo-tongs that have rubber covered tips. Never use sharp metal tweezers that could injure the mouth. After preparing fish, always wash your hands before reaching into the snake's cage, and never handle fish with gloves that are used for picking up your snake. Water snakes include frogs in their natural diet and some will accept toads or even other snakes. It is best, however, to keep all water snakes on a fish diet because frogs, toads, and snakes

Because all snakes will bite at some time, the beginner should never attempt to keep or handle a venomous snake. Accidents always happen. *Bothrops alternatus.*

demand a lot of attention if you are going to maintain a supply during the long winter months. Water snakes emit an offensive musk whether they are handled or not; good ventilation is a must.

Some snakes that make excellent pets feed almost exclusively on live toads. These include all of the hognosed snakes, familiar snakes that are short and stout and virtually never bite. The only prob-

Sea snakes are venomous, virtually unobtainable, and unkeepable. If you should see one offered, avoid it. *Hydrophis klossi.*

lem here is that you may find it very difficult to maintain a supply of toads for winter feeding. This problem will often force you to place your pet into a false state of hibernation by placing snake and cage in a cool, dry, dark place for the duration of the winter months. However, you must make sure that your pet eats heartily so it can build up some fat reserves before subjecting it to a false state of hibernation. The best way to assure survival of your pet is to return it to its natural habitat prior to the snake's natural period of hibernation. Hognose snakes will sometimes feed on live frogs and insects.

Rodents such as mice and rats are the preferred food of many kinds of beautifully patterned and interesting snakes. However, less than 30 percent of these snakes can be trusted as pets. Kingsnakes and the rosy boa are the really docile snakes of this group. Many of

your rat snakes will adapt pretty well to a caged life, but they are unpredictable when it comes to biting.

After six months of handling without a single bite, some will for some unknown reason or another suddenly bite, and then may not repeat this for another six months. Gentle handling does not seem to be the key factor. Others, like the gray and the yellow rat snakes, are not to be trusted because, unless captured when young, they have a nasty disposition. Other rodent-eaters that are of the same nature, but more so, are the racers, coachwhips, whipsnakes, and pine snakes. All of these snakes strike with great speed and will bite any part of your body that is available at the time of their decision to do so. However, because of their diet of rodents, this group of snakes is easy to raise. Mice and rats can be purchased at your local pet shop all year around, or you can raise your own with very little trouble. For the health and safety of you and your snakes, never trap wild rats or mice for your pets—they often harbor serious parasites. Many of your rodent-eating snakes will also feed on other snakes, and some will even eat frogs and lizards.

An albino specimen of the California kingsnake bred in captivity. Such specimens fetch a high price but are worth it. *Lampropeltis getulus.*

Many of the rat snakes, *Elaphe,* make good pets. Old World species, such as this *E. quatuorlineata,* often appear at reasonable prices in pet shops and may be suitable for the more experienced beginner.

HOUSING

From the standpoint of any animal there is no such thing as a perfect cage, but to make the cage as livable as possible there are several things for you to consider. First, it must be escape-proof or you will be very unpopular with not only members of your household but equally so or more with your neighbors. It must be understood that the following suggestions for keeping snakes as pets apply only to non-poisonous snakes. Snakes are experts at finding some loose section of screening or a weak corner of their cage, and it is amazing how small a crack one can squeeze through. Make certain first that the cage is escape-proof.

The most popular form of cage is a rectangular box with a clear plexiglass or standard glass front and half wood and half soft screen cloth top. The top, which is the entrance to the cage, may be hinged or slide. The sliding top is preferred among snake enthusiasts. Either of the two, however, is better than a side door that swings open, as too many snakes escape while the door is being opened. To provide additional ventilation, a 2- to 3-inch opening should be made near the top of the back of the cage and covered with soft screen cloth.

All screening should have the cut edges on the outside of the cage and should be secured with wood screen molding and brads. Some snake keepers glue the screen and molding to the cage and then nail it before the glue sets. Be sure that you use a good grade of screen cloth. By no means do you use metal screening, because an active snake will soon have a sore nose. All snakes seem to spend most of their captive life searching for a way out, rubbing and pushing their nose against every square inch of their cage. For easy cleaning, the glass front should be removable. With a little extra work that is well worth it, you can even provide a sliding metal floor.

The size of the cage will depend on what kind and size of snake you want to keep as a pet. A cage for a garter snake or any

FACING PAGE: Snakes from tropical countries often require more elaborate terraria than do North American species. *Rhinobothryum bovalli* from Central America.

18

Snake cages can be made at home, although if you only need a few they are more readily purchased. This bank of cages was made for breeding kingsnakes.

other species of snake that is about 2 feet long should measure about 15 inches high, 24 inches long, and 15 inches wide. A cage as small as 10 inches by 14 inches by 10 inches is large enough for small garter, ringneck, or green snakes, while for larger king, black, or rat snakes a cage about 20 inches high, 36 inches long, and 20 inches wide is ample. Your snake needs enough room to crawl about freely, and the height should be sufficient for the captive to climb vertically as well as horizontally.

Many snakekeepers use an aquarium as a cage. I personally find only one advantage in using a glass aquarium: it is easy to clean. The problems with glass are that it is difficult to hinge a door to, there is very little air circulation, and temperature control is not good. If you

decide to use one, I might suggest one of two-gallon capacity for a snake 12 to 24 inches in length; ten-gallon for over 24 to 36 inch snakes; and 20-gallon capacity for over 36 to 48 inches. This doesn't mean to say that you could not use a larger tank than suggested. After all, regardless of the size of a snake, it will make use of all the room you can afford to offer it.

Cage Props
When it comes to dressing up the interior of a cage, be sure you have the snake's safety, comfort, and habits in mind. Do not put in a lot of rocks or branches, because too much dressing will cut down the space needed by the snake to move around. One thing to remember is that although a crowded cage may look exactly like the snake's wild habitat, you are the one who has to clean the cage. Most important is a water dish. This should be large enough for the snake to crawl

Water, light, heat, and shelter are the basic requirements of all snakes.

into, for many kinds of snakes like to soak themselves for hours at a time. A weighted plastic dog food dish is the best because it cannot be overturned by the snake. The water dish should be kept clean and at all times filled with clean water.

You will probably want your snake visible so that your friends can see it, but again, think of the snake and provide a retreat of some kind where the snake can go for a rest. You can always remove the retreat from the cage when your friends are really interested in seeing the snake. A flat stone propped up by some pebbles or a rough slab of bark to crawl under will do for a small snake. For a large snake a small box with an opening at one end should be provided. A cardboard shoe box or some other such container that can be replaced when it becomes soiled is best. A short section of a hollow log is also very good, but it could become a cleaning problem. I prefer to construct a lightweight, flat-topped wooden retreat because you will find that the snake seems to like coiling on the top of its retreat.

Many snakes like to climb, so you may want to place a short section of a heavy branch into the cage. This will provide a roving ground as well as a resting place for your snake. It will also present the opportunity for you to observe how a limbless creature moves about the branches of a tree. A small shelf at one end of the cage near the top or a dowel rod running the length of the cage will give you the opportunity to observe many examples of snake gymnastics.

Always keep in mind that cleanliness is just about the most important issue with snakes, as it is with any kind of pet housing. Remember, a dirty cage breeds bacteria that may cause illness and even death to your pet. The cage should be cleaned regularly and occasionally scrubbed with a weak ammonia solution. Snakes can be placed in snake bags during the cleaning period, because cages should be thoroughly dried and aired before returning the snakes to them. After scrubbing cages and props, I usually spray them with Lysol disinfectant and then let them dry and air out. This is a good time to inspect your snakes for parasites and other health problems so that they may be treated before returning them to their cages.

Temperature

Temperature control is very important to snakes because they are cold-blooded creatures, which means that their body temperature is not much higher than the temperature of their surroundings. If the temperature of an area where the cage is being kept averages 75 to 80°F you should have no problem. However, if the temperature is much below 75° you can provide heat by placing an electric light

If properly designed and maintained, the snake terrarium can be the focal point of the room.

bulb in or near the cage. Depending on the size of the cage, you might have to experiment with different wattage bulbs until you find the one that will average out the temperature between 75 and 85°F. When using a light bulb, always keep a thermometer in the cage at all times. A bulb inside the cage does not have to be covered, but make sure that no electrical wires are exposed to the snake.

Many snakes, especially those that live where extreme cold winter conditions prevail, hibernate for their protection during this season. If you happen to maintain a specimen from such an area, it may decide to honor the time of hibernation, regardless of the temperature maintained within its cage. When this happens, the snake will become listless and refuse to eat. If the snake is in good health it can go for months without food. If during this time the snake is kept in an area that maintains a constant average temperature of 40° to 50°F, it should be covered from all light and not be fed. With the arrival of the spring season, the snake and its cage can be returned to preferred activity temperatures, and it should accept food as usual.

FEEDING

Probably the most difficult part of keeping snakes is getting them to feed. Many, like the rat, pine, and gopher snakes, usually accept food without problems, while others, such as milk snakes and black racers, commonly refuse to eat. All snakes are flesh-eaters, and they ordinarily eat food that they kill themselves. However, after some time in captivity, a snake that is a good eater can often be induced to take dead prey such as frozen, completely thawed mice offered with the aid of a pair of long, rubber-tipped darkroom print tongs and kept in motion until the snake grabs it.

Many family members and friends will probably object to feeding live animals to a snake. "It's cruel." You might explain to them that the feeding habits of all flesh-eating animals are necessarily cruel, even their purring cat or the robins in the back yard. There is probably no quicker or more merciful death than that of a mouse attacked by a constricting snake. The mouse is observed sniffing curiously at the snake, showing no sign of fear, when suddenly the reptile strikes and the rodent practically disappears from view, concealed in the snake's coils. Death is almost instantaneous, and it is certain that the mouse never knew what happened. It is certain that the rodent suffered less than if it had been grabbed by a house cat, dog, or been struck over the head with a stick.

It is not necessary to feed a snake very often. One meal a week is a good schedule, and many snakes are satisfied with one good portion every two weeks. However, smaller snakes that feed on insects and earthworms can be fed every three or four days. There is no real danger of over-feeding your snakes. All snakes can be depended upon to stop when they have had enough.

All live food should be placed in the snake's cage during the early evening and left all night. Most snakes are more likely to feed when things are quiet and nobody is watching. If the food has not been eaten by morning, remove it, wait a day or two, and then try again.

If your snake refuses to eat after several attempts and you are certain it needs to be fed, you will have to try force-feeding. Be-

FACING PAGE: The problem with buying a rare or unknown snake is that you never know just how to keep it and feed it. *Lycodon striatus bicolor.*

cause it can be traumatic to the snake, force-feeding should be considered a last resort. One method of force-feeding is to hold the snake behind the head, force its mouth open, and gently but firmly force a pink (young) mouse or a piece of fish or frog (depending, of course on the species of snake) down the snake's throat. Be very careful not to break any of the snake's teeth, as this could lead to serious mouth infections. It might help if the food is pre-moistened with water or, even better, cod-liver oil; it will not hurt the snake. Be careful not to use large pieces of food, even though the snake's throat is quite elastic. With the food part way down the throat, give the snake a chance to swallow it voluntarily. Should the snake refuse to cooperate, massage the lump of food gently, rubbing it above and away from the snake's head, until the food goes down. Repeat this procedure until you are satisfied that the snake has had a substantial meal.

Another method is to purchase some large, empty gelatin capsules from your pharmacist, fill them with chopped mouse or ground fish (hamburger is too fatty for snakes), and force one down

This rainbow boa feeds well on mice, which makes it relatively easy to care for. Mice of all sizes can be purchased all year long. *Epicrates cenchria.* When feeding live rodents, be careful—if left overnight in a snake's cage, they may attack the snake.

Snakes with specialized feeding habits are often impossible to feed during the winter. How do you get toads for a hognose in January?

the reluctant snake's throat. A more sophisticated method is a large syringe or caulking gun with a long plastic surgical rubber tube. The tube should be soft and tapered at the end that enters the snake's mouth. Fill the syringe or caulking gun container with the proper finely ground food and attach the tube, which should be from one-quarter to one-half inch in diameter and 6 to 10 inches in length, depending on the size of the snake. Before inserting the tube into the snake's mouth and throat, coat it generously with cod-liver oil or pure petroleum jelly. Insertion of the tube must be slow as to not injure the snake's throat. Squeeze the plunger slowly until the desired amount of food is injected, then remove the tube slowly as your fingers close the throat behind it. You may want to force the food toward the stomach by rubbing your thumb along the bottom of the snake's neck to the stomach, which is located about one-third the distance from the head to the base of the tail.

Because force-feeding can be injurious to the snake, it is seldom worth attempting unless the specimen is too valuable to lose. Na-

Rat snakes such as this *Elaphe obsoleta quadrivittata* usually feed well in captivity. If you have to force-feed a snake, it is probably best not to keep it in captivity.

tive snakes are best released into their native range rather than trying to force-feed them.

You may want to mix up a balanced diet for your snakes, such as adding an egg, one teaspoon of cod-liver oil, and four to six drops of multivitamin formula to your finely ground meat. If the snake is ailing, this is a good time to add medicine to its diet.

When force-feeding small or very young snakes, use chicken or beef blood mixed with a couple of drops or multivitamins and feed with a medicine dropper inserted into the small snake's throat. However, many small snakes will become dependent on force-feeding and will never eat on their own. Always keep trying to encourage these snakes by offering them their preferred live food, and only force-feed if absolutely necessary.

Cage Sharing

You can keep more than one snake or more than one species of snake in the same cage, providing you use care in selection. Some species eat other snakes, so you must keep these separated from other snakes. The snakes most apt to dine on other snakes include, among others, kingsnakes, black racers, pine snakes, gopher snakes, milk snakes, and some water snakes. Such snakes will often kill and swallow other snakes larger than themselves.

Great care should also be taken when feeding more than one

snake in a cage, because while one is attempting to swallow its food another snake may begin swallowing the other end of the prey and eventually the other snake. It is best to feed each snake separately. A separate cage with a clean wooden floor (no props) and a water bowl is fine as a feeding cage. Place the food in the cage first and then the snake. Leave them alone and undisturbed until the snake feeds, then give it another half hour or so before returning it to its regular cage. This is a very good feeding method because it is easy to keep a feeding record of those snakes that are caged together.

Large, aggressive species, such as this Asian mangrove snake, *Boiga dendrophila*, require their own cage and a great deal of care in handling.

GENERAL CARE

Always remember that, regardless whether you purchased your snakes or took them from their natural haunts, they are your responsibility. Treat them with consideration and always think of them as being your guests, rather than your captives. Keep their cages warm, not hot, feed them regularly, and keep their quarters clean, and you will have and enjoy snakes as pets for a long, long time to come.

Teasing not Allowed

Some of your friends may be thoughtless at times, waving their hands about close to the glass front or knocking on the glass in order to tease them into striking. Freshly caught snakes, especially black racers, and water snakes, will strike savagely when tormented, and it will not take long for a snake to develop a painful bruise on its nose or dislocate its jaws. It goes without saying that if you intend to acclimate your snake to a caged life you will not stand for this kind of cruel treatment. If you don't want to get unpleasant about this by telling your friends off, notify them before showing your pets. Better still, place a sign on the top of your cage that reads, "Please do not tease the snakes. Thank you."

Handling snakes

Always handle your snake by holding it just in back of the jaws so that it cannot turn and bite. At all times approach a snake from above, never from the reptile's own level, and always with slow, deliberate movements, never quick and jerky. After a while the snake will realize that it is not going to be hurt when it is being handled, and it will struggle less and less. When the snake has calmed down you can gradually release the neck hold and permit it to crawl from one hand to the other and through your fingers and around your neck. In a surprisingly short time many snakes will show no evidence of fear or anger when you pick them up and may even seem to enjoy being handled. Just a word of caution: most large water snakes, all racers and coachwhips, gray and yellow rat snakes, and some pine snakes should never be trusted and may never take to handling.

FACING PAGE: Beginners should avoid large snakes with questionable dispositions, such as most pythons. *Python reticulatus.*

The mouth of any snake should be kept a safe distance from your face, as a mere blink of an eye, movement of a lip, or the breath from your nose or mouth might induce the snake to bite one of these areas. Again, all bites should be washed thoroughly and treated with a good antiseptic immediately after they occur. The bites of large water snakes should be watched carefully in case they have become infected.

Shedding of Skin

Snakes that hibernate during the cold winter months or estivate during the hot summer months shed their outer layer of dead skin two to five times a year. However, in the southern United States and points south the hibernation and estivation periods are very short, and some young snakes may shed eight to 12 times a year. (Older snakes shed less often than young ones as they are growing much more slowly). Your captive snake, if young and healthy, may shed its skin

When the skin of a snake begins to appear dull and milky, shedding is probably about to commence. *Helicops carinicauda.*

every six weeks or so. Estivation is much the same as hibernation, but takes place during extreme hot weather. Both are forms of suspended animation, where all body functions, including the heartbeat, are slowed down to a minimum.

The first evidence that shedding is near comes when your snake's eyes become clouded, bluish white in appearance, and the snake acts as though it were going blind. Other signs include sudden inactiveness, irritability, and refusal of food. After a time the snake will begin to rub its chin vigorously against a branch or stone. Eventually the skin will break at this point and the snake will literally crawl out

The snake frees its head from the old skin by rubbing its snout and jaws on a rough surface.

of it, turning it inside out as it does so. If there are plenty of stones, branches, and other rough surfaces in the cage for the snake to crawl and rub against, it should have no problem shedding, but sometimes a captive snake requires a little help. If the old skin sticks to the snake in places, like around the head area, it may be necessary to soak the snake in water for a brief period of time to help loosen the old skin. You could use your fingers or tweezers to remove the stubborn patches of skin, but only do so as a last resort, as you could damage the

new skin. Most snakes are surprisingly docile and tolerant while you are working on them. After shedding has been completed the snake will be at its very best, both in shining color and alertness, and will usually be ready for a hearty meal.

Breeding in Captivity

By providing ample cage area, ideal temperature, and proper food for male and female snakes of the same species and approximately of the same size, you may encourage reproduction. It is sometimes better to have more females than males because males will very

The tail of a male snake is usually much broader at the base than that of a female snake; male snakes also tend to have longer tails than females.

often breed with different partners during one mating season. Most temperate zone snakes breed every year or every other year, usually during the spring; snakes from the tropics may breed several times a year. The first hint of mating is the courtship routine displayed by the male, who gently rubs his body, especially the nose and chin, against the body of the female. When this action takes place it is best for anyone observing them to keep out of sight of the participants. The lights of the cage or room should be slightly subdued, movement kept at a minimum, and definitely no sudden noises. The slightest interference of any kind may discourage the potential mating pair.

This female indigo snake, *Drymarchon corais*, has laid a clutch of eggs that are being incubated on vermiculite in a sweater box. Young of many snakes can be hatched and raised in captivity.

When collecting your specimen during the late spring or early summer months, you may collect a pregnant specimen that will give birth to living young or will lay eggs to be hatched by some form of incubation. Except in extremely rare instances, the female shows no interest in the eggs or young once they leave her body. Should you be confronted with this situation, special care of the eggs and young is necessary.

If your pet lays eggs they can only be hatched with proper care. Do not attempt to recreate nature's plan by placing the eggs in dampened soil, sand, or vegetation. Because of the lack of proper air exchange and natural accumulation of moisture, the eggs could mold and spoil. Eggs should be placed in an open dish with damp, not soaking wet, paper towels under and over them. Constant temperatures of 70 to 85°F should be maintained, and the covered eggs should be placed in an area where they will receive good air circulation. Do not keep them in direct sunlight. Keep paper towels damp and check eggs daily for any signs of mold. If mold spots appear they may be gently rubbed off with a cotton swab dipped in isopropyl (rubbing) alcohol.

When a snake is ready to hatch it will cut a slit in the leathery shell by means of a tiny "egg tooth" and then crawl out of the egg. The egg tooth is shed shortly after the snake hatches. When hatched, the little snake is an independent animal, and you can either release it in the wild (exactly where the mother was caught) or you can attempt to raise it yourself.

In the case of livebearing snakes no special preparations are necessary. However, the young should be removed from any parent snakes that are considered to be cannibalistic. Young snakes must be watched very closely to make sure that they are feeding properly. Small crawling insects and their larvae are a good source of food. Nightcrawlers and small frogs will also be taken by some species. In the case of water snakes, strips of freshwater fish flesh or small guppies or minnows can be placed in a saucer of water and offered to the baby snakes.

By much selective breeding in captivity, kingsnakes have been produced in numbers in many types of patterns that are very popular with keepers. This is a normally patterned California kingsnake, *Lampropeltis getulus californiae.*

Releasing Your Snake

If for some reason you have to give up your snake, do not give it to another person without making certain that he or she has some knowledge of snakes and the work involved in caring for them. If your friend has little or no knowledge, explain what you know and what you have learned while keeping snakes as pets.

If, however, you choose to release your pet, make sure that it is released in their natural habitat and definitely before their hibernating period, which depends upon the location in which you live. Try to release the snake where it was caught, certainly never more than a few miles away. When releasing snakes in the temperate zone make

One advantage of keeping locally collected snakes is that if you should have to get rid of them it is not difficult to release them where you found them.

sure that the weather is warm and winter is yet to come, no later than early October, and never release any specimen that is not native to your area of the country. For instance, if you have a southern hognose snake from Florida, do not release it in Illinois. Never release a snake that is from a foreign country. Many states have strictly enforced laws that prohibit such releases. Also, foreign snakes will almost always die if released into a strange habitat. Some snakes, in order to guarantee their survival, should be returned to the wild, if only for these two reasons: (1) your inability to maintain warm, comfortable quarters for your snake during the cold, winter season; (2) your inability to maintain a constant food supply, especially for those snakes that feed on toads, insects, and earthworms.

YOUR SNAKE'S HEALTH

By Terry L. Vandeventer

Anyone making the decision to bring a wild animal into captivity must be aware of the fact that this animal, having now been removed from its natural environment, will be susceptible to any number of health problems. The problem may have been with the animal already or it may develop upon entering the captive state. On the whole, reptiles are a hardy group and thrive in captivity if provided with only a few of their most basic needs. Occasionally, however, health problems do crop up, and it is the pet keeper's responsibility to see that his ward is cared for properly.

Many ailments in captive snakes can be avoided beforehand, while others present us with a live-and-learn situation. Reptilian medicine is a relatively new field and much still needs to be investigated. Large collections like those found in zoos are more susceptible to rare diseases and odd injuries simply because of the sheer numbers of individual animals being dealt with. In the private home where only one or a few snakes are kept, the chance of your pet "catching something" is slight.

Snakes, like all living reptiles, are termed "ectothermic" (cold-blooded). This means that they must rely on outside sources for their body temperature. Each species has a preferred optimum body temperature at which they function best. In the wild a snake will remain secluded on days too hot or cold for its liking. Low temperatures render the snake virtually helpless, with slowed bodily functions. Extremely high temperatures, on the other hand, are avoided because of the danger of overheating. In order to reach a happy medium, a snake will alternately bask in the sun and move to the shade. In this way it can avoid too much of either extreme and keep a rather constant body temperature.

In captivity the correct temperature must be provided and maintained to ensure feeding and proper digestion. The right level of warmth is also mandatory in order for the snake's system to provide

FACING PAGE: Small burrowing species with specialized requirements should not be kept by beginners. *Sonora episcopa.*

defenses against diseases. Most North American species thrive best at 76° to 85°F (24.4. to 29.4°C). Temperatures upward of 85°F (29.4 C) should be carefully avoided.

One of the most common ailments of captive snakes is respiratory infection (R.I.) stemming from the cage being kept too cool. R.I. is characterized by wheezing, excessive mucus in the nostrils and mouth, and heavy, labored breathing through the mouth. The snake may take very deep breaths, making the entire body appear bloated. The breath may be held for quite a while then finally expelled with a long hiss, only to be drawn again. Untreated cases are often fatal.

R.I. can be treated by reinstating the proper temperature, perhaps just a degree or two warmer during the period of treatment. Medication can be given orally (in the food or by tube) or by injection. Chloromycetin (15 mg/kg), Ampicillin (3-6 mg/kg), and Tylosin (25 mg/kg) are usually effective within a week or so. In addition, the use of multi-B vitamins and vitamin C seems helpful.

Occasionally the snake may continue breathing through the mouth after the condition seems better. This is due to dried mucus left in the nostrils, and the condition will clear with the next shedding of the skin.

Any number of disorders may result from keeping your snake too cool. Another such problem is that of intestinal enteritis. This is recognized by vomiting and diarrhea. The stools of a healthy

Pliocercus elapoides is an unusual species in that it can drop its tail much as can an anole. Such natural wounds heal quickly.

snake consist of dark fecal material and white, chalky uric acid. In a snake suffering from enteritis the stools are clear, loose, and the solid material is off-white and gelatinous. In severe cases the snake may pass these bad stools several times per day and weight loss may be drastic.

As in any ailment of a reptile, you must be sure that the proper warmth is once again achieved and maintained. Take away the water bowl for three or four days and at the end of that time replace the water with a solution of Neo-Terramycin powder. This medication comes in a four-ounce package and can be found at farm supply stores or be purchased from your vet. The dosage is somewhat difficult to calibrate, but ½ tablespoon to 1½ pints of water has been very effective. By depriving your pet of water for a few days it will be more

The snout of this garter snake, *Thamnophis sirtalis,* is not badly abraded, which means that it is either a recent captive or one that does not constantly try to escape by rubbing along the walls of the cage.

likely to drink readily when the medicated water is introduced. Provide a fresh solution daily until the condition clears and vomiting stops. Neomycin sulfate is the active ingredient of the medication and is available in many forms.

After feeding, a snake will usually pass a stool about three days later and another after a few more days, depending on the size of the meal. Each species and individual varies. If you are worried that your pet may be constipated, a simple warm water soak (from a few minutes to overnight) will almost always stimulate a bowel movement. Gentle manual massage also helps.

As a rule, snakes fare best in a dry environment, and even water snakes usually need no more than a small bowl of water to be content. In fact, these semiaquatic snakes are the most susceptible to a moisture-related condition known as "blister disease." This ailment results from excessive moisture and poor sanitation in the snake's cage. Even water snakes must dry off, and if confined in such poor conditions will develop blisters and eruptions on the skin.

Water snakes enjoy coiling in the water bowl, thereby causing it to overflow. At shedding time many snakes do this. While the cage should not be allowed to remain wet, the snake may need the soaking naturally. At other times, however, the bowl should be replaced with one just large enough to supply plenty of drinking water and not allow bathing.

To treat blisters, the cage must remain perfectly dry. The blisters can be carefully drained and swabbed with hydrogen peroxide or a mild antiseptic. Provided that the cage is kept very clean and dry, the blisters should disappear with subsequent sheddings.

A snake may develop ulcerations on the gums along with swelling and excessive salivation. Untreated, the infection invades the deeper tissues and bone and is fatal. The mouth of the snake should be carefully swabbed twice daily with Sulmet, Betadine, or hydrogen peroxide. The yellowish ulcerations may be debrided (cleaned out) or left intact; sources differ in their opinions. Injections of Tylosin or another broad-spectrum antibiotic in conjunction with multi-B vitamins and vitamin C are effective. The snake should be provided with fresh, clean water daily during this period, and treatment should continue until the gums are healed.

Ectoparasites are a scourge that every reptile keeper has experienced. Ticks are simply removed with forceps and the wound treated with iodine. Until recently the snake mite, a black, pin-head sized blood feeder, was not as easily managed. Snake mites *(Ophionyssus natricis)* appear as tiny black specks all over the snake, especially between the scales and around the eye. Dead mites are usually found drowned in the water bowl and may be first evidence of an infestation. These little mites do not infest people but can cause dehydration in small snakes as well as serious skin and blood diseases. Household pest strips (plastic strips impregnated with an insecticide) are excellent for killing and controlling mites. A small piece (about 2 inches square) should be placed in a jar equipped with a perforated top. Place the jar in the snake's cage. In this way the vapors can circulate but the snake cannot come into direct contact with the strip. Leave the jar in for about three days, then remove it. The remainder of the strip can be

hung in the room normally. These pest strips are very effective against mites and seem to be completely harmless to North American snakes (if properly used), although their use with very small snakes should be monitored closely.

Small flukes often inhabit the mouths of frog-eating snakes. These flat black trematodes usually present no problem but can be removed manually if desired.

As mentioned earlier, snakes kept in captive conditions may exhibit problems not normally encountered in the wild. One such example involves difficulties with shedding the skin.

If it is certain that your snake is overdue to shed, you will need to offer some assistance. The skin will become dry, crackled, and wrinkled, and some may already be separated from the body. Soak your pet overnight in a shallow, warm bath. The skin may readily come off by itself or you can shed it through your hands. Always be sure that the transparent eye caps come off with the skin. If not they may come off with the next shedding. Either way, they cannot be allowed to remain. Blunt forceps work well, as does a piece of cellophane tape, for removing old eye caps.

These are only a few of the ailments that may befall a pet snake, but they represent those most commonly seen. As reptilian pets gain popularity, more veterinarians are being consulted on their health problems. Many vets, just like most people, are not particularly enthused by snakes and may refuse the case. More, however, are researching the subject and accepting the challenges. You may wish to contact a professional if your pet's problem seems more serious than what you can handle personally.

Unlike some infections and diseases of mammals and birds, the infections and diseases of snakes are nontransmissible to humans—another very good reason for selecting snakes as pets. Parasites such as ticks, mites, and some nematodes (unsegmented, cylindrical worms; roundworms) are transmissible to humans. Cleanliness is the key word to health.

Wild-caught snakes, such as this Mexican kingsnake, *Lampropeltis mexicana,* often have mites and ticks.

Common and Banded Water Snakes

Heavy-bodied snakes with keeled scales and dorsal crossbands. Average length is about 30 inches (76 cm). There are many variations in color among specimens from different areas of North America. The most common subspecies of the common water snake, *Nerodia sipedon,* found throughout most of the northeastern part of the U.S. southward to southern Tennessee and west to Kansas and Oklahoma, usually has a ground color of pale to deep brown, with maybe a tint of red. On this ground color is a dorsal pattern of brown crossbands, broader on the back and narrowing on the sides. Toward the tail, however, the bands tend to break into blotches. The underparts are mottled with drab gray and black, sometimes with touches of red. The banded water snake, *Nerodia fasciata,* from the southern United States, is very similar to the northeastern species but the bands extend the full length of the snake's body and it displays more red in the pattern. The underparts are yellowish, brightly spotted with black and red. Range of this snake extends from coastal North Carolina to the southern tip of Florida and west to Texas. Old individuals, regardless of locality, generally lose their bands or have only slight indications of them and become almost uniform brown in color.

Frogs and fishes are the main choice of foods for this snake; however, when not available, crayfishes and salamanders can be substituted. A banded water snake will forage mostly during the night and will very seldom stray far from the water, its avenue of escape. When first encountered it will strike viciously and is capable of inflicting a serious wound with its sharp, slightly curved teeth. It is a wound that should be treated with a good antiseptic.

A good place to search for these water snakes is along the shoreline of slow-moving rivers, quarries, lakes, ponds, swamps, and drainage ditches, especially among the low branches of trees and

THE BEST PETS

FACING PAGE: Although beautiful, the green tree python is not suitable for keeping by beginners—or even by most advanced hobbyists. *Chondropython viridis.*

shrubs that overhang the water. The best method of capturing them is with a noose at the end of a cane pole, the same equipment used for capturing the out-of-reach, elusive lizards. Hunting at night from a boat with the aid of a flashlight will, almost always, prove successful.

Like all water snakes, these species when disturbed will give off an offensive odor produced by secretion contained in the musk glands, located just under the anal plate. However, once captive they will very seldom use this offensive measure unless frightened. Captive specimens more often than not become adjusted to handling and breed regularly when given clean, dry housing with constant temperatures.

Banded and common water snakes bear living young late in the summer months. The average litter is about 25, but litters of up to 44 individuals have been recorded. The approximately 8 inch (20 cm) hatchlings are brightly patterned. They will bite, and their musk glands are well developed at birth. During August and early September young banded and common water snakes, along with other local species of water snakes, can be found during or right after heavy rainfalls on roads paralleling rivers and drainage ditches.

Brown Water Snake, *Nerodia taxipilota*

A strongly keel-scaled, heavy-bodied, blotched brown snake that has an average length of 42 inches (107 cm). The range of this snake extends from southeastern Virginia through eastern North and South Carolina over most parts of Georgia and all of Florida to extreme southeastern Alabama. The background color is reddish, almost rusty brown, and there is a mid-dorsal row of darker brown, squarish blotches. On each side is a row of similar but smaller blotches that are separated and alternate with those of the middorsal row. Old specimens are usually dull brown with but a mere trace of a pattern. The head is wide and well distinct from the neck. The tail tapers abruptly. Because this snake somewhat resembles the deadly cottonmouth (water moccasin) and shares the same range and habitat, one must be sure of positive identification before any attempt is made to capture it.

Lakes, rivers, swamps, ponds, and drainage ditches are the preferred habitats of the brown water snake. It enjoys basking in or out of the sun's warm rays probably more so than any other water snake. It is a social snake that can often be observed basking on the same object with others of its kind. It is a good climber and can often be seen basking among the low branches of a bush or tree that overhangs the water. Although escape is this snake's first choice, it will, when molested, stand its ground and strike savagely at the intruder.

Its bite is nasty. Fishes, frogs, salamanders, crayfish, and even small turtles are eaten by this snake.

The brown water snake gives birth to living young, usually during the month of August. Coloring of the young is much brighter than that of the parents. Ten to 15 young make up a litter. The length at birth is about 10 inches (25 cm).

This snake is usually hardy in captivity and will generally accept food readily. Some specimens become very used to having people around them and may even take to handling. It lacks the ferocity of some of the other water snakes, but remember that both jaws are armed with sharp, curving teeth that can produce serious skin lacerations.

The common garter snake, *Thamnophis sirtalis,* is perhaps the best snake for the beginner—common, cheap, colorful, and hardy.

Common Garter Snake, *Thamnophis sirtalis*

A keel-scaled, striped snake that is considered common throughout its range; average length about 22 inches (56 cm). This snake has a range that includes almost all of temperate North America. Coloration is an olive brown background with three distinct longitudinal yellowish stripes. It displays considerable variation in color and in details of the spotting and checkerboard pattern on the dorsal surface between the three distinct stripes. As in the other garter snakes,

one stripe runs down the middorsal surface and one runs along each side of the body. The head is the same color as the background (but may be reddish out West) and the lip or labial plates are the same color as the underparts, greenish or yellowish; there is often some narrow black edging near the ends of the ventral plates. Just described is the most common combination of color and pattern. The stripes on some specimens may be brownish, greenish, or bluish. Some individuals may even be without stripes. Sometimes the spots or checkering may be more prominent than the stripes and vice versa. Often red is present between the stripes, and the entire upper surface of the head may be bright red.

Although this species seems to favor moist situations, it can often be encountered in all kinds of habitats: forests, open fields, backyard gardens, roadsides, vacant property next to human dwellings, parks, or close to a body of water. It is found under all kinds of debris: tires, boards, pieces of cardboard, newspapers, flat stones, and in empty tin cans and other containers. The food of this garter snake consists of earthworms, frogs, toads, tadpoles, crayfishes, salamanders, an occasional fish, and associated insects. Only on rare occasions does it eat warm-blooded prey, young birds and mammals. When first encountered it is aggressive and will strike viciously at an intruder, but escape is its first choice. A large specimen is capable of inflicting severe skin lacerations and should therefore be handled with respect. However, as a rule, a specimen that is held for five minutes or so will usually calm down and is not likely to bite again. Garter snakes are particularly noted for the scent or musk glands that are located at the base of the tail. When irritated, the snake is prone to discharge a strong, foul-smelling secretion from these glands, but once in captivity this is very seldom ever repeated.

The garter snake gives birth to living young. A litter may contain as many as 50 young that are able to crawl to safety immediately after birth. The young resemble their parents.

As a captive, the garter snake is very hardy and will accept nightcrawlers, smaller worms, frogs, and tadpoles. Some will take crayfish or minnows that are placed in a small container of water. Because of the musk situation, good ventilation should be considered when constructing a cage for any species of garter snake. Garter snakes will breed in captivity when given peace and quiet and a clean cage with proper props. The very young can be fed small earthworms and mealworms to ensure them an adequate diet.

Eastern Ribbon Snake, *Thamnophis sauritus*

A slender, keel-scaled snake with three longitudinal stripes

that bears a strong resemblance to the common garter snake, which is relatively stouter. There are several species and subspecies of ribbon snakes that are well distributed throughout North America, but the most common with the largest range is the eastern species, *T. sauritus.* The range of this snake extends from the central part of New England to Lake Michigan and southward to eastern Louisiana and the western half of the Florida panhandle; one of its subspecies occupies most of Florida. The average length of this snake is about 18 inches (46 cm). The background color varies from gray to greenish black. Like the common garter snake, with three longitudinal stripes, one middorsal and one on each side of the body. These stripes are usually bright yellow, but the middorsal stripe on some specimens may have an orange or greenish tinge. The underparts are yellowish to yellowish green and unmarked. The head is quite small, with a narrow vertical yellow mark in front of each eye.

The eastern ribbon snake occupies all kinds of habitats but is almost always found close to water. Unlike the garter snakes, the eastern ribbon snake is not too fond of earthworms but will feed upon frogs, tadpoles, small fish, and salamanders. Most of this snake's hunting is done during the daytime in the moist, tangled grassy edges of swamps, ponds, lakes, rivers, and drainage ditches. However, it can be encountered both day and night under all sorts of debris, rocks, and logs. It is very fond of water and is an excellent swimmer that generally keeps to the surface with its head out of the water. When frightened it will, however, submerge, and usually takes refuge among aquatic plants. It is capable of staying under water for as long as five minutes.

It is a very nervous, excitable snake that seldom becomes docile when handled. However, its teeth are too tiny to inflict serious bites, although large specimens can draw blood. Captive specimens seem to remain in an excited mood and will almost always attempt an escape when the door or lid of their cage is opened. When a captive, it can become very hardy and will eat even leeches and chopped fresh fish.

Ribbon snakes, like garter snakes, reproduce by live birth. A litter averages about a dozen individuals that are exact duplicates of their parents. Aquatic insect larvae are their first choice of food until they are large enough to take tiny frogs and salamanders.

Hognose snakes, *Heterodon* spp.
Heavy-bodied, keel-scaled snakes that have upturned noses. Average length is about 24 inches (61 cm). The range of the eastern

Heterodon platyrhinos, the common species of hognosed snake, is almost impossible to feed during the winter because it needs a diet of toads.

species *(H. platyrhinos)* extends from New Hampshire southward through Florida and westward to Minnesota, Oklahoma, and Texas. Coloration of this species may be gray or yellowish brown. On the dorsal area is a pattern of irregular squarish blotches of dark brown or black. There are smaller blotches on the sides that alternate with the dorsal blotches. The underparts are yellowish green, with black spots at the edges. Some may have dark grayish to almost black underparts, and some specimens may be entirely black with little evidence of a dorsal or side pattern. There is usually a dark band in front of the eyes and a band that extends from the eyes and ends at the angle of the mouth. From the first two blotches on the neck there are two broken lines that extend to the top of the head. A keel on the rostral (nose) plate gives this snake an upturned, shovel-like snout.

The range of the southern species *(H. simus)* extends from Virginia southward to Florida and west to extreme eastern Louisiana, all south of the mountains. Smaller but stouter proportionately than

the eastern species. The dorsal surface and sides are usually pale gray, never black, and red may be included in the pattern. The underparts are unmarked. The southern species seems to prefer dry flood plains, wire grass flatwoods, brushy fields, and fruit groves or orchards.

The western hognose (*H. nasicus*) is a species of the Great Plains that ranges from Alberta, Canada, well into Mexico. The characteristic that separates this species from the other species is the presence of a largely black belly that is interspersed with white or yellow (the other species have light bellies). Within its range this snake inhabits dry, open prairie areas, especially those with a sandy surface.

No description of habits of a hognosed snake would be complete without mentioning the outstanding trait of the genus. When persistently annoyed the snake will turn onto its back and writhe in seeming agony. After a short while it will become quiet, but remains on its back with the mouth open and the tongue hanging out. It will remain in this position as though dead, and if picked up it will hang limp and motionless. If turned onto its belly it will flip over quickly

This view of a hognosed snake shows the pointed snout used for burrowing and digging up toads.

onto its back. This writer once picked up a feigning specimen and put it in a child's swimming pool, where the snake floated on its back and remained motionless for five full minutes. When picked up and put back on the ground on its belly, the snake quickly flipped over onto its back. A death-feigning hognosed snake will only move after the intruder leaves.

Toads are the main choice of food of all hognosed snakes. As most of us know, toads have a powerful skin poison that kills or sick-

ens most predators, but hognosed snakes are immune to toad poison. The protecting substance apparently is a secretion of their greatly enlarged adrenal glands. These snakes have large, lance-like teeth in the rear part of the upper jaws. These teeth are used to deflate the toads, which try to prevent predators from swallowing them by puffing up their bodies to two or three times their normal size. As soon as the snake swallows enough of the front part of the toad's body, it punctures and deflates the toad with its large rear teeth. Despite the ability to spread their necks cobra-like, hiss loudly, and strike viciously, they are in reality very docile snakes that always strike at an intruder with closed mouths. Hognosed snakes are often encountered crossing a field or back yard in search of food. Frogs and some insects are also eaten by these snakes. The upturned snout is used for burrowing and for digging up toads.

Hognosed snakes reproduce by laying eggs. Ten to as many as 30 eggs are deposited under forest or field debris. Hatchlings are marked like the parents but are slightly more gray in color.

Hognosed snakes take readily to a captive life, and once adapted to their cage they will eat toads and accept handling. However, they have the tendency to lose their habit of feigning death.

Racer, *Coluber constrictor*

These smooth-scaled snakes are, without a doubt, one of the most common snakes over virtually all the United States. Only the common garter snake can compare in abundance. The average length of a racer is about 48 inches (122 cm). There are several subspecies that are all slender snakes with satiny color above whether black, blue, or greenish, and black to white below. Snakes from the eastern U.S. are glossy black above and below, usually with a white chin. In the Mississippi Valley the racers tend to be bluish with whitish to yellowish bellies. Out west they are greenish tan with yellowish bellies. The young are banded and look vaguely like slender rat snakes.

Racers tend to be very nervous in captivity, and many specimens never adapt. They feed largely on small mammals and birds. Not recommended for beginners.

Coachwhips, *Masticophis* spp.

Coachwhips or whipsnakes are considered to be the fastest of all North American snakes. The average length is about 66 inches (167 cm). The eastern coachwhip *(M. flagellum)* record length is 102 inches (259 cm). This particular species is found from North Carolina south to Florida, and westward to Colorado and New Mexico. Coloration of the eastern subspecies is yellowish brown, with the head and

the first few inches of the body dark brown to almost black. The underparts are pale in color, shading to yellowish near the tail. The smooth scales over the posterior part of the body and the entire tail are arranged in such a manner as to give the impression of a braided buggy whip. Another six or so subspecies occur in the western U.S. and Mexico. The most often-seen subspecies is found from Colorado through western and central Texas as far south as central Mexico. The coloration of this subspecies is yellowish brown to dark brown, without the dark head and neck. Crossbanding on the neck may be present on some individuals.

Other coachwhips of the western states may be reddish in coloration, and some have longitudinal stripes. All, however, have the braided buggy whip characteristic.

Habits of all whipsnakes are very similar, both in temperament and in feeding habits. All are very pugnacious when their safety is threatened. When threatened, these snakes will vibrate their tail rapidly and will strike repeatedly at all intruders. Coachwhips will accept food when held captive and not disturbed too much, but they never seem to lose their fierce disposition and will resent handling as long as they live. Gloves should be used when handling adult whipsnakes. All are capable of delivering a serious lacerating bite that should be treated immediately with a good antiseptic.

Coachwhips feed on small mammals, birds and bird eggs, lizards, and occasionally other snakes. They are not constrictors. They are egglaying snakes that lay 12 or fewer elongated white eggs.

The braided scales of the coachwhip, *Masticophis flagellum*, earned it its common name.

Pine Snakes, *Pituophis melanoleucus*

Pine snakes *(Pituophis melanoleucus)* are large snakes with an awesome hiss and are always ready to strike at anyone who comes near them. Average length is about 50 inches (127 cm). Their range extends from New Jersey to eastern Tennessee and southward to Florida and Alabama, with an odd black subspecies in southern Mississippi and adjacent Louisiana. There is a very closely related species in an isolated area that extends from the eastern part of Texas to central Louisiana *(P. ruthveni)* that is referred to as the Louisiana pine snake. Except for the black pine snake, all others compare quite closely in coloration and pattern.

Northern pine snakes have a dorsal surface that is grayish white, gradually grading to almost pure white on the sides. The dorsal area has a series of black blotches that are very distinct on the posterior portion of the snake but run together to become less defined toward the head. Small black blotches are very pronounced against the very pale sides. The blotches on the anterior part of the body and entire tail take on a dorsal-barred appearance. The underparts are grayish white, marbled with black. The head is comparatively small. The Florida subspecies is an almost uniform brown or grayish brown with faint dorsal blotches. The Louisiana pine snake has dark blotches that are most pronounced on the posterior part of the body and are often reddish in color. The black pine snake is black or dark brown and may or may not have evidence of a pattern on the back and sides. All pine snakes have keeled scales.

High pine country with sandy areas is the chosen habitat of all pine snakes. They will, however, travel across open fields when foraging for food. Pine snakes are powerful constrictors that prefer warm-blooded prey: mice, rats, and other rodents, as well as rabbits, birds, and their eggs. Large eggs are not swallowed whole; instead, when the egg enters the snake's throat the snake presses this portion against the ground and then contracts the muscles of the throat to crush the shell.

All pine snakes have a nasty disposition and are always ready to defend themselves against all intruders. However, escape is their first choice. When irritated, a pine snake will face the intruder and raise the forward part of its body until the head is high off the ground, then take an enormous breath and expel it with a loud, prolonged hiss. During this defense attitude the tail vibrates rapidly. Its strike is extremely accurate, and the jaws and sharp teeth are capable of delivering a nasty bite.

Pine snakes lay from six to 12 rather large eggs. The hatch-

The pine snake,
*Pituophis
melanoleucus,* is a loud
hisser but seldom bites.

lings are vividly patterned; across the face they have a dark, mask-like line very much like that of a raccoon. The body blotches are a rich chestnut brown.

Some individuals take to captivity and careful handling. These will take many foods, including small chicken eggs (preferably those purchased directly from a chicken ranch—not candled). However, specimens that do not take to captivity should be released in the area from which they were taken.

Bull Snake, *Pituophis catenifer* and *P. sayi*

Sturdily built, strong, and agile snakes with an average length of about 60 inches (152.4 cm). They can be found in the Great Plains area from Canada to Mexico and from Indiana and Wisconsin to the Rocky Mountains. They are most abundant in Arizona and Texas. Bull snakes are sometimes referred to as gopher snakes (especially *P. catenifer*) in certain parts of their range. All are, however, related to the pine snakes. All bull snakes prefer open plains, prairies, and sand dunes wherever there are concentrations of brush and warm-blooded animal burrows.

Coloration is yellowish brown to orange brown with a series of more or less square medium brown or black blotches on the dorsal area and a row of paler, much smaller blotches on each side. The underparts are yellowish and blotched with black. The head is rather small and somewhat pointed, suggesting the snake's burrowing habits.

Bull snakes are constrictors that feed entirely on warm-

blooded prey such as rats, mice, ground squirrels, prairie dogs, and rabbits. When available, birds and bird eggs are also eaten. Captive specimens have been known to eat frogs. When first approached, these snakes will attempt to defend themselves vigorously, vibrating their tails, hissing, and striking savagely. However, soon after capture they will calm down and become docile and good-natured snakes that can be handled with ease. They are ideal snakes for the fancier and lecturer.

Bull snakes are egglaying snakes. Ten to 20 eggs about the size of a small chicken egg are deposited under a log, stump, or rock pile. Hatchlings are about 15 inches (38.10 cm) in length and resemble the parents in coloration and pattern.

Bull snakes are very beneficial snakes that help to check injurious rodent populations. They will enter a rodent burrow and wipe out entire families. To aid the population of bull snakes, only one or two specimens should be taken for your collection.

Eastern Kingsnake, *Lampropeltis g. getulus*

A snake that averages about 40 inches (102 cm) in length. It is a smooth, glossy-scaled snake that has a black background color with narrow white, sometimes yellow, crossbands that fork on the sides and unite with one another to form a chain-like pattern. Dorsal scales in the black areas may have a light central dot. The underparts are checkered with black or brown and white or yellow. Some southern specimens have a background color of brown instead of black.

The range of this subspecies of the common kingsnake extends from central New Jersey southward east of the Alleghenies through North and South Carolina, Georgia, most of Florida, and southeastern Alabama. Numerous other very similar subspecies occur over the western and central parts of the United States.

Although associated with dry and forested areas, this kingsnake has been observed in marshy areas foraging for frogs and entering the water voluntarily to swim across rivers and ponds. It is not a very good climber and therefore spends most of its time on the ground, hiding under logs during the hot daylight hours. It is a powerful constrictor that hunts for small mammals, ground-nesting birds, and all kinds of snakes and lizards. It hunts during both the day and night. Although an aggressive snake when attacking prey (it will strike readily at humans when cornered), it will calm down rather quickly and soon becomes remarkably docile when handled. Of course, no snake can really be trusted, and it always should be handled with care.

About a dozen eggs are laid during the summer, commonly

among the roots of some decaying stump or under a mossy log. The young are patterned like the parents.

Yellow Rat Snake, *Elaphe obsoleta quadrivittata*

This is a slender snake with stripes and slightly keeled scales. The average length is about 48 inches (122 cm). The range of the yellow rat snake extends from Cape Hatteras, North Carolina southeastward through South Carolina, Georgia, and most of peninsular Florida. Most specimens are pale yellow to olive yellow or pale yellowish brown, with four dark brown stripes extending the length of the body, two on the back and one on each side. The stripes may be quite indistinct on some specimens and very prominent on others. The underparts are pale yellow. The head is paler than the upper body and is without stripes. The tongue is black.

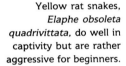

Yellow rat snakes, *Elaphe obsoleta quadrivittata*, do well in captivity but are rather aggressive for beginners.

The yellow rat snake prefers woodlands and brush-covered fields. It is an excellent climber, nearly always ascending the branches of brush or trees to rest or to digest a meal. In fact, the great majority of individuals will be observed among the branches of trees and bushes. It commonly invades barns and old deserted buildings in search of rats and mice and enters chicken coops for the same purpose; it is not adverse to taking chicks and chicken eggs. In these locations the yellow rat snake can often be found resting in a coiled position among the rafters. Food consists of warm-blooded prey. Rats and mice and other small mammals usually make up the bulk of its diet,

but small barnyard fowl and their eggs are taken when the opportunity occurs. This snake has a great fondness for eggs. With its superb ability to climb, during the nesting season this snake takes a heavy toll of birdlife. Young birds, rats, and mice as well as small eggs are simply swallowed, but larger prey is constricted before being swallowed.

The yellow rat snake can be a very aggressive snake, but if there is any way of escape it will usually retreat in an unhurried manner. If challenged, it will put up a bold and courageous fight. The head and neck will be raised well off the ground as the snake faces the intruder, the tail will vibrate rapidly, and, when approached too closely, the snake will strike viciously and repeatedly until it can escape or be subdued.

The yellow rat snake lays about two dozen eggs during late June and early July. They are usually deposited under a fallen decayed tree, rotted stump, or debris. Hatchlings are about 12 inches (30 cm) long and are marked quite differently from their parents. They are dull gray in color with a series of darker gray or brown blotches on the back. At the age of one year the yellow background color will appear and the characteristic four-lined pattern will become obvious. From then until they are about two and a half years old they will reveal the patterns of both immature and mature specimens. The snake will mature at the age of three years old.

The majority of specimens eventually become fairly tame and feed readily on small rats and mice. However, they cannot always be trusted when being held or when placing an object in their cage. Gloves should always be used.

Corn or Red Rat Snake, *Elaphe guttata*

This very attractive rat snake has an average length of about 35 inches (89 cm). Its range extends from New Jersey and Maryland southwestward through North and South Carolina, Tennessee, Georgia, Alabama, Mississippi, Louisiana, and the extreme southeastern part of Texas, with a much duller subspecies found from central Texas and the Great Plains into Mexico. This snake has a background color of reddish brown to gray. The dorsal area is patterned with a series of large, bright red blotches that are outlined with a narrow border of black. There are two rows of smaller, less brightly colored spots on each side that alternate with those on the back. The first blotch on the neck divides to form two lines that extend forward and meet between the eyes. A brownish red stripe with dark borders extends from the eyes across the brow and backward past the mouth, terminating on the neck. The underparts are white and strongly patterned with

The corn snake or red rat snake, *Elaphe guttata,* makes an excellent pet for the more advanced beginner.

square black patches. As with so many other snakes, old individuals are often faded and duller in color. Hatchlings have dark reddish brown blotches with patches of orange between them running along the middle of the back. The pattern is much brighter than that of the parents. Numerous albinos and other color forms of the corn snake are now bred in captivity.

This snake prefers sandy pinelands, flatwoods, brush-lined fields, and old buildings. It is a strong constrictor that hunts mainly at night and is seldom observed during the day. The daylight hours are usually spent resting under a log or in the fork of some tree. An excellent climber, it will ascend to the highest branches of a tree that offers it a nest of birds or their eggs. However, the main diet includes all kinds of rodents, especially the rats and mice that begin their destruc-

Because of their diet of soft-bodied insect larvae, rough green snakes, *Opheodrys aestivus,* are difficult to keep successfully.

tive foraging at the same time that the red rat snake goes hunting. It will not hesitate to enter cellars, wood sheds, barns, chicken coops, or any other outbuildings likely to harbor mice and rats. Rather bolder than most nonpoisonous snakes, it will often refuse to escape even when given the opportunity. It does not attack, but very commonly a surprised specimen will stand its ground, assume an attitude of defense, and dare a person to come closer. Although many individuals become "tame," it can never really be trusted as much as the kingsnakes. It becomes a hardy captive and will accept food, especially mice and sparrows, with little hesitation.

Green Snakes, *Opheodrys* spp.

There are two kinds of green snakes that inhabit the United States. The smooth green snake *(O. vernalis)* has smooth scales and averages about 18 inches (46 cm) in length, while the rough green snake *(O. aestivus)* has keeled scales and averages about 28 inches (71 cm) in length. The range of the smooth green snake extends from Canada to southeastern Saskatchewan and the Rocky Mountains, south as sporadic colonies to North Carolina and Texas; it is absent from the southeast. The range of the rough green snake extends southward from Connecticut to Florida and the Gulf States, northward in the Mississippi Valley to Kansas, Illinois, and Ohio. The smooth species is more terrestrial in habits, while the rough species is more aboreal. Coloration of both species is the same: uniformly delicate iridescent leaf green above, devoid of any pattern, the underparts whitish to yellow or yellowish green. The tail is very long and tapers sharply to a pointed tip.

Although the smooth green snake is mostly terrestrial, it will sometimes ascend branches of bushes to rest in safety or forage for food. The rough green snake is an excellent climber and spends a large part of its time among the branches of bushes and trees, where its harmonizing color matches the foliage so perfectly that the snake is almost impossible to see.

Insect larvae, spiders, and other soft-bodied invertebrates are the main food for all green snakes. They are very docile snakes that can be handled with safety from the moment they are caught. They never display a bad temper and rarely attempt to bite. In captivity, grubs and other smooth, soft-bodied larvae are readily accepted by these very slender bright green snakes.

Green snakes reproduce by laying eggs. Four to 12 very elongated eggs are deposited under a flat stone or rotting log, usually at the edge of a grassy field near trees. The eggs are usually found

adhered to one another in pairs. Hatchlings are grayish green to pale, delicate green.

Boa constrictor, *Boa constrictor*

Because of convenience and availability, North American snakes have been the subjects discussed throughout this book. However, because the most common of all pet store snakes are the boa constrictors of South and Central America and many pet keepers may want to purchase one as their first snake, this popular species is included. This is not done to encourage commerce in an exotic species,

Boa constrictors, *Boa constrictor*, are one of the few exotic snakes that can be successfully kept by beginners. Very young specimens are fragile and seldom survive long in captivity, so look for small adults.

but rather to help us see that those that are imported do survive.

These South and Central America boas have both the common and scientific names the same—*Boa constrictor*, the boa constrictors. They seldom exceed 12 feet (3.6 m) in length, and the average length in the wild state is about 6 feet (2 m). As their common name implies, they are powerful constrictors that feed almost exclusively on warm-blooded prey (although juveniles may take the lizards and insects). They are attractive snakes that vary so much in pattern and coloration that they are somewhat difficult to describe. However, the most handsome type is the red-tailed boa, whose back is patterned with broad, elongate, saddlelike, pale gray blotches on a background color of rich chocolate to almost chestnut brown. The sides are some-

what paler in color and are patterned with dark brown spots that are often diamond shaped, with light centers. The tail is brightly marked with brick red and white. The underside is yellowish, spotted or dotted with black.

Boa constrictors are excellent climbers and are very fond of water. Although their habits are largely nocturnal, they are often observed foraging during the daylight hours. Food consists of monkeys, peccaries, rabbits, and all kinds of rodents and birds. Some individuals have been observed feeding on large tree lizards, such as the green iguana. Juveniles of course eat proportionately smaller prey than adults.

These snakes are usually docile and mild-mannered, seldom displaying any signs of annoyance when being handled. It is suggested, however, that when a beginner buys a boa it should be not more than about 3 feet (1 m) in length. Even a specimen of this size is capable of inflicting a painful and dangerous bite that should be treated immediately with a good antiseptic or antibiotic salve. Specimens under about 3 feet in length, on the other hand, are delicate and subject to many illnesses.

Captive boa constrictors are excellent feeders and will survive very well on a diet of laboratory mice, rats, and rabbits; some will take small chickens. The cage should have ample room, a good size water dish, and a heavy branch for climbing and resting and to aid the snake during the shedding period.

Boa constrictors bear living young. Litters are large and may contain upwards to 30 individuals. Length of a newborn is about 24 inches (61 cm). The pattern resembles that of the parents. Young boas will feed on all kinds of small mammals and even lizards and large insects.

An adult boa constrictor in good color is a beautiful snake. Some specimens have better temperaments than others, but few are very aggressive.

The following books by T.F.H. Publications are available at pet shops and book stores everywhere.

ENCYCLOPEDIA OF REPTILES AND AMPHIBIANS—By John F. Breen
ISBN 0-87666-220-3;
TFH H-935
576 page; 267 color photos; 316 B & W photos

SUGGESTED READING

Fine introduction to the world of living herps. Covers both native and exotic snakes in detail, with information on natural history of most species commonly kept in captivity. Section on feeding live foods. Non-technical.

BREEDING TERRARIUM ANIMALS—By Elke Zimmermann
ISBN 0-86622-192-4; TFH H-1078
384 pages; 175 color photos; numerous line drawings
The best book available on captive breeding of herps, including commonly kept snake species, both native and exotic. Must reading for the serious hobbyist. Moderately technical.

SNAKES AS PETS—By Dr. Hobart M. Smith
ISBN 0-87666-908-9; TFH AP-925
160 pages; 51 color photos; 55 B & W photos
A standard reference by a prominent American herpetologist on collecting and keeping North American snakes as pets; heavily illustrated, with many western species. Non-technical.

PYTHONS AND BOAS—By Peter J. Stafford
ISBN 0-86622-183-2; TFH PS-846
192 pages; 111 color photos; 22 B & W photos plus numerous line drawings
The best coverage of the popular pythons and boas. Must reading for every hobbyist with even a passing interest in the group. Excellent natural history and care sections with many species (common and uncommon) illustrated in color. Moderately technical.

BOAS AND OTHER NON-VENOMOUS SNAKES—By Werner Frank
ISBN 0-87666-922-4; TFH KW-002
96 pages; 27 color photos; 53 B & W photos
Good introduction to captive snakes, with emphasis on diseases and easy to keep species. Non-technical.

Index